# My Beginning

susan mokh

BookLeaf
Publishing

Presentation by *BookLeaf Publishing*

Web: www.bookleafpub.com

E-mail: info@bookleafpub.com

ISBN: 978-93-95890-40-3

First edition 2022

# DEDICATION

I of course would like to thank everyone, but specifically my father for his sacrifices, love and his belief in my abilities. He is the reason I write.

# ACKNOWLEDGEMENT

I thank BookLeaf Publishing for giving me this opportunity.

# PREFACE

Naked truth, honest thoughts, and the questions I was afraid to ask and answer.

# Angel Cry

Final heartbeat rang through the sweat on my
skin
Leaden bottle fell as my world faded in a spin
The chance of a tomorrow washed off quiet
shore
I sheathed my sorrow, for death the victor of my
war
I was greeted with white as been told in many
lore
The voice of angel bellowed shaking my very
core
I froze bewildered at this ethereal sight
Then tear of an angel prompted my greatest
plight
I knew I blundered in allowing misery reign
For the woe of an angel the heaviest of rain

# Deep Feeler

My mind a scatter of a myriad of thought
Heart quakes with pain and fraught
My lips pretermit the shadow of smile
And soul hath morphed to nature of vile
I have become a distortion of my past
My mask askew plumbs reactions aghast
Thus retorsion of isolation probes no doubt
Whilst laws of morale I proceed to flout
I pray my thoughts find their way to rest
Lest my life of happiness remain of divest

# Goodbye

3

I have been on this ledge for far too long
The wind's echoing a foreboding song
Staring at the abyss in awe and fear
Ruminating when my life had become a drear
I pray for strength in aid of my cower
Whilst the voices in my head grow louder
They tell me to jump to my eternal rest
With the promise of worries falling egest

# One Minute

I sat there with you in honest bliss
A feeling I believed forever I'd miss
The lyrics I sang and to the music I swayed
I cried and prayed this moment remains
unscathed

Though with dawn comes a brand new day
And thus my content had faded away
We discovered a journey that halted to end
Causing despair in which eternity I'll spend

# You

5

I have never known a love so potent
One that mends all that was and shall be broken
A love that shames the vast world of fiction
And renders "I love you" to feeble diction

I had never believed my soulmate I'd find
A man that knows no end to being kind
A love that encompasses family and friend
And promises our story shan't ever end

I have yet to wrap my mind around
How our love is so ethereally profound
And marvel at our level of relation
A paramour that elicits my ecstatic elation

I have never loved as I love you
And vow to forever remain so true
I pray our adoration never falters
And someday we'll be standing at the alter

# I Hate You

The words I wrote were of strife
Not one blessing saved my life
Submerged in heartache and sorrow
I lost sight of the hopeful tomorrow

Whilst I drowned in deepest despair
Of your ethereal presence unaware
A bystander to the shatter of mine own heart
You were collecting the scattered parts

Thence you emerged with your heart and mine
Gave me your own thence my life redefined
Under your spell of perfection I was struck
And due to your devoted love I am eternially
stuck

# The Villain

I have contemplated the fatality of sin
For they say evil could never truly win
The villain is shunned and abhorred
And for haven he can't even ask the lord

Morality is made to be of utmost import
Thence the hero warrants all's support
For he who fights in the name of propriety
Wears the bloodshed in a crown of piety

Though I believe the paragon and ruffian are on
par
For both wear gallantly their battle scars
Although one brawls in the name of the people
Who's to say the other knows not but evil

# Faded

The appeal of sunsets no longer prevails
And the words I write are of no avail
The stitch of sanity torn at the seams
I can no longer fathom childlike dreams

Life has drained me dry of it's own
Left me with but bruises to be shown
However I marvel at it's ethereal power
As it churns the brave making them cower

I have become but a shadow of mine past
Abyss of lonesome hath grown so vast
I no longer crave being blissfully elated
For my being has morphed to one so faded

# Words Of Last

9

I like my kin fear our inevitable sleep
And futilely hope this life forever we'd keep
Though death it looms and poses threat
It is not responsible for my constant fret
I walk on eggshells with the words I say
Lest I pass with relations gone astray
Thus "I love you" accompanies goodbye
And "I'm sorry" I'll say even when a lie
Alas that is how I live and shall my remaining
days
For life is fleeting and death will have its way

# Final Goodbye

It is not the lies, I no longer crave
Nor the fact that you had dug my grave
It is not due to the sleepless nights
Or the endless, countless fights
And although your kindness I never did know
And my tears I had no time to stow

You were never worth the time I spent
And you left and left my life unkempt
But the reasons prior and the more unsaid
Are not what prompted my burning our thread
What truly forced me to walk away...
I-Alas- have fallen in love with one who
promises to stay

# The Man That Never Was

We met over coffee on a winter day
And although in a hurry I decided to stay
As such we talked till hours ticked to years
Till we let go of all our worries and fears
But who would've thunk this all would change
My life you'd alter and to the worst rearrange
Thereafter you left with your heart and mine
Left me to wonder if I'll ever be fine
I guess that posits- I was your just because
Whilst you to me were the man that never was

# I Loved You

12

We were sprawled out, gazing at the stars
Giggling at the extent of our par
The stories we told prolonged our night
And we marvelled at how we never did fight
In your presence my joy would overflow
And in mine your smile forever held its own
For this I thought our love shan't falter
Thus I began to picture my gown and the alter
Whence abruptly you stood shaking with tears
And suddenly my body ceased with fear
You knelt and whispered your final goodbye
Your words of last- a string of your finest lies
The many of stars thus dwindled to a few
For what you said had sounded like I loved you

# Suicide Note

My life-though short- has filled with pain
Inflicted upon I, and I was a bane
For this I've decided-this life I'll flee
Perhaps the next may be of great decree

'Tis selfish I am painfully aware
Grief shall rain upon those who care
But those who don't will suffer most
Memories of hurt shall morph to ghost

Ink shall tattoo my final thoughts
An image of my own distraught
My story- the myriad of reasons why
I have solemnly chosen for myself to die

I'll bid adieu to all, in manners of discreet
For I cannot openly admit to defeat
And quietly and rapidly walk away
I've dug my grave, 'Tis time to lay

# My Words

I write about heartache and pain
Find solace in the pouring rain
I depict the stories of present and past
Fall in love with what shan't last
I illustrate the prodigious heft of my heart
Wonder if misfortune will remain my chosen
form of art
I compose lyrics embedded with tears
Hoping to rid myself of my numerous fears
I compile all my ifs, buts and why
Smoking ink- the words are my high
I iterate what my heart desires
Stand by, whilst my soul's set on fire
I inscribe syllables of grief upon my skin
The curse of a poet, promises a life of no win
I write consistently and continuously
Heart bleeding words quite vigorously

# Your Story

15

Your name no longer sketched in pain
Happiness I need not feign
After long, you and I have become
Alas third chances granted to some
In a state of skeptic ecstasy
For your loss will have no remedy

# Stuck

16

The things I want to do I can't
The words I have to say, I shan't
The barriers placed are of mine own
I guess we all must reap what we have sown

# Little Towns

17

The twinkle of star light,
The early morning dew
Kids flying kites
Golden innocent hue

The towns are of paper
The sky always blue
No leader a dictator
No room for taboo

The sun always rises
Masks fall askew
Unraveling lies
Allure of little towns are untrue

# Once Again

Standing on the rooftop screaming your name
Hate and it's opposite emanating from the heart
you've maimed
Wishing I didn't and hoping it had
Perhaps then it wouldn't have hurt this bad
But all "great" things must come to an end
And I'm not okay, but I will have to pretend
Regardless, and despite I must let you walk
away
And hold my tongue when my heart begs you to
stay

# Letting Go

19

Some nights it all comes crashing down
The flash of an image- myself in a hospital gown
And I wonder if it truly matters, and if I should care
The bottles waiting- calling- do I dare?

# Forget Me Not

Forget me not I told you as you lead me down
the stairs
You shook your head and smiled, said you will
always care
Forget me not I asked as you helped me with my
coat
You turned away and laughed, suggested I write
a note
Forget me not I begged while getting into bed
You turned the light out and said "not even if I
lose my head"
Forget me not I whispered as my memory
flickered off
You held my hand and squeezed, "how could I"
you scoffed
Forget me not you cried and begged of me to
stay
I touched your cheek and smiled, as I blinked
my life away

# Forgotten

In a box so dusty, I sneeze at the thought
Is a mass of items that had been left to rot
From first grade, to first kiss, and all between
The parties the dances, my life as a teen
The heartache, the mistakes and all the sorrow
The heartbreaks that made me forget about
tomorrow
The coffee, the sunshine, the rain and snow
The long hugs, the goodbyes, the highs and the
lows
The fist bumps the high fives and the endless
chatter
The clubs, the games, and forgetting what
matters
A lifetime of memories were left in that box
Forgotten and dusty, but as stealthy as a fox

www.ingramcontent.com/pod-product-compliance
Lightning Source LLC
LaVergne TN
LVHW010023200726
843495LV00015B/1911